FINDING LOVE AGAIN

ELLA MORGAN

REDSTONE BOOKS

First published in 2013 by Redstone Books

British Library Cataloguing-in-Publication data
A catalogue record for this publication is available from the British Library

ISBN 978-0-9560898-1-6

Printed and bound by CPI Group (UK) Ltd, Croydon, CR0 4YY

Cover Image ID 13723862 Courtesy of www.dreamstime.com
Image registered to www.redstonebooks.co.uk

This book is dedicated to Dennis for his constant encouragement and for sharing our compassion and love for Dodi

CONTENTS

PREFACE

In 2010 we saw an advert on the Internet asking for a home for an elderly disabled dog – a Shih Tzu called Dodi. Only his face was visible in the advert and he looked so sad.

Dodi was totally deaf, partially sighted and about thirteen years old, he had been found in his home guarding his owner's dead body which had lain undiscovered for many days, possibly as long as seven days.

According to the rescue centre, the police team who found Dodi had thought he was in such a skeletal state that he should be 'put to sleep' as a kindness. However the local rescue organisation agreed to try and find him a home. Unbeknown to us his little advert had appeared on the Internet for nearly a year before we saw it. No-one wanted such an elderly disabled dog needing significant veterinary treatment. We thought we could give him a couple of years of unconditional love in our home in the Cumbrian countryside. We made the call.

Dodi has been with us for just over two years. He survived all his treatment including some tricky dentistry that removed most of his bottom front teeth and he is now a happy and playful roly-poly teddy bear of a dog. Studying his behaviour we realised that he clearly had been loved before, he took to the attention we gave him 'like a duck to water'. He had mannerisms, likes and dislikes that told us a lot about his previous life. He had certainly lived with an elderly owner who had a well established routine. He barks in the right room to tell us things, he 'looks' towards what he wants, or at the person who normally gives it; and 'puts down his anchors' when he doesn't want something. He was certainly used to being spoilt particularly in terms of sleeping late in the mornings and often on our bed! He preferred cheap dog food or better still, human food and he liked that food little and often. He just loves routine and gets distressed if something doesn't happen 'on time'. This latter preference was the most difficult to ignore or change so we have worked around it. If the routine activity really can't be done, then he gets a special cuddle instead; this has worked remarkably well and we don't now have to go to bed every night at 9pm!

What happened to him could happen to any pet. A beloved owner can die suddenly and circumstances and coincidences may conspire to cause a horrible delay in other people finding out. This is not deliberate negligence but a pet is so dependent on the maintenance of the 'status quo' as far as his owners are concerned. Pets are particularly vulnerable if someone has an accident when they are out, or as in this case suddenly dies. Pets cannot really care for themselves if they are 'home alone.'

'Finding Love Again' is a *story* and apart from us and Dodi, the characters are entirely fictional. I have tried to imagine how events could have worked against his discovery. He was not neglected by his owner, but he became vulnerable after her death only because assumptions were made by others. We should all be vigilant about our elderly neighbours particularly those with pets.

'FINDING LOVE AGAIN'

Chapter 1: Nora

Nora looked around her small tidy kitchen; she had loved this little terraced house so much; more when William was alive but still now when she was here alone. She glanced at the shining surfaces, the rows of 'Willow Pattern' cups and plates on the dresser, the neat pine cupboards and gleaming red linoleum. Nora had always been tidy, even as a child she had liked order and '*a place for everything and everything in its place*'; it was her mother's rule that she had maintained because it seemed so sensible. This ordered way of life had helped William a lot when he became blind, he had remembered where everything was, so could easily negotiate furniture and room spaces and of course it never changed. Now that model was helping Dodi.

Nora looked across at the soundly sleeping little dog who had been their pet for 11 happy years. They had both loved him as soon as they saw him at the dogs' home; that was so long ago now when he had been just a puppy. He was the runt of the litter, smaller and shyer than the rest of the boisterous puppies who leapt at any visitor like small fluffy monkeys. This little chap just walked slowly around people's legs sniffing them. The dogs' home guardian explained that the breeder had gone out of business, being shut down because of lack of proper care for the dogs. This litter had been brought to the shelter by the RSPCA. The little black, white and brown puppy was totally deaf but otherwise seemed ok. Other visitors hadn't wanted to take a 'disabled' puppy so he was still available. Nora and William looked at each other – they had intended getting an older dog but this little one seemed to need them so much. The guardian told them that he probably was a Shih Tzu, or perhaps a cross with a Lhasa Apso another Tibetan breed. William bent down to pick him up and he snuggled into his shoulder, it was an adorable action. After completing all the forms required by the shelter, they took him back to their home.

William and Nora were staunch Royalists and like many older people they had adored the Princess Diana, she could do no wrong in their eyes. When she had visited Manchester they had made the bus trip to stand in the street and watch her pass by, William was sure that she had looked right at him and waved madly, but then so had many other people in the crowd! Even when it appeared that Diana was about to marry an Arab gentleman this had not put William off and so when they brought the puppy home he said that he had been thinking about a good name for him on the bus back – Dodi; and it seemed just right.

Nora snapped out of her reverie – these days she often found herself dreaming of times past, especially times with William. She and William had been married for 57 years when he died. He hadn't really been ill in all that time. He did have diabetes but it was well managed with insulin and they were used to any limitations that placed on him. In later life he became blind first in one eye and then the other, one of the things that happened to some diabetics. At the end he had caught pneumonia which was difficult to treat because of his diabetes. She had cared for him in their spotless home right to the end. A tear welled up in her eye at the thought and she brushed it away. No use crying now, she was on her own and she had to make the best of it. She was lucky she had good friends, she was warm and well fed and she had Dodi. They got along together well, especially now that the cat next door had moved away!

When Dodi had been about 9 years old, they had moved to their present home, a house owned by William's nephew. A young family lived next door – they had seemed nice enough, the young man was a welder and his wife worked in the local Co-op store; they had two young children and a black and white cat. They were friendly and the little ones often came into 'Aunty Nora's' for a drink and a chat after school. Nora liked the old fashioned way that the parents had with the children, expecting them to call their neighbours 'Aunty' or 'Mr and Mrs', not the first name terms that many children seemed to use these days; it showed a level of respect which William and Nora liked. When William had become ill the young woman had helped Nora out with shopping or collected things for them from the chemist in town, she was kind and thoughtful, not so her cat.

'Basher' lived up to his name, he was bad tempered and spiteful and Nora wouldn't let him in the house.

He roamed her garden as if he owned the place and one awful day he attacked Dodi. Dodi had not heard him crashing through the tall border plants towards him, he looked up at just the wrong moment and Basher slashed his paw across his face. Dodi yelped and ran for home. He hurtled through the kitchen door and fell panting to the floor. William heard the commotion and hurried into the kitchen; he picked Dodi up and saw that his left eye was already closed. The young woman next door was horrified, she had heard the squeal and looked out of her window to see Dodi hurtling towards his house with Basher in hot pursuit; she scrambled through the gap in the fence and found Nora and William comforting Dodi. She immediately offered to run William to the vet in the town. Nora phoned first to warn them and William, cradling Dodi in a blanket, and his neighbour set off in her little car. Dodi had to be tranquilised in order for the vet to take a proper look at his eye. Sadly she pronounced that the slash had caused a lot of damage to the surface of the eye, it would partially heal but might not ever recover fully; his sight would definitely be significantly impaired. William was horrified. Poor Dodi totally deaf and now partially sighted. They drove home in silence; William wondering how to tell Nora, and his neighbour feeling so guilty about her cat.

The next door family were very upset, but everyone agreed that it was just an accident; you couldn't blame a cat for behaving like a cat. Nevertheless it altered the friendship and somehow even the children felt a sense of guilt over Dodi. When his eye started to heal, he could open it again but his sight was very poor in that eye. William joked with the children that now both of them were half blind, one in the right eye and one in the left eye, perhaps they should be tied together like a '3 legged race' so that they could both use their good eyes! The children dutifully laughed at the joke but they looked at Dodi sadly as if somehow it was their fault. A month or so later the family moved away taking Basher with them, and the house was empty for some time. Eventually a young woman moved in who was out at work all day and Nora barely saw her.

Nora's house was really the end of a terrace, although it was joined to the archway that linked the next bit of the terrace and provided a little alleyway that led to the back gardens of the houses. Nora's neighbour across this little lane was Mary, a widow who was about the same age as her, over the past couple of years they had become reasonable friends, sometimes popping into each other's houses for a cup of tea, or just talking across the alleyway. Mary wasn't fond of dogs or they might have done more together but Nora and William would never leave Dodi for a whole day so outings were out of the question. Occasionally after Williams death they would go into town on the bus together and Mary always tried to pop in or at least talk to Nora once or twice a week, they had both agreed that this arrangement would make sure that each of them was looking out for the other since they were both alone in the world.

Basher the cat had moved at about the same time that William's condition took a turn for the worse, the diabetes started to affect everything. He would cut himself shaving or working in the garden and the wounds wouldn't heal properly, then the cataract in his right eye became inoperable and the left eye started to show signs of a new cataract developing. William and Nora went out as often as they could; William wanted to get a good dose of 'visions of nature' before they were completely lost to him. They visited parks and stately homes on the bus, went on coach trips and train rides to gardens and the seaside, castles and forests. Dodi got very used to the travelling and the special walks at the end of the journey, there were always interesting smells and William and Nora always took a packed lunch so that they could sit outside with him. On their way home Dodi slept on the seat between Nora and William and became a perfect traveller.

'Time I stopped dreaming Dodi and got on with me ironing,' Nora said.

Dodi snored peaceably and took absolutely no notice.

While Nora was ironing she remembered that she had to feed the electric meter, she had brought back lots of appropriate coins from her visit to the paper shop on the way back home from town and she had stuffed them in her apron pocket when she took off her coat; where they were now clanking away while she smoothed sheets, pillowcases and handkerchiefs. She reached into her pocket and put the money in neat little piles on the edge of the dresser nearest to the little cupboard where the meter was. As soon as she had finished the ironing she meant to load up the meter. It was very useful having a meter, no nasty shocks when the bills came in. The house was owned by her nephew, who appeared about once a fortnight to cut the grass for her and she paid her rent directly into his account through the bank. Other people in the street believed that she owned the house as they did theirs; but no, it was Darren's house and she and William had rented it from him for the past few years. It meant that they could live very comfortably off their pensions and did not have any building maintenance to worry about.

When the neighbours saw Darren arriving with his lawn mower or ladders and tool box they just thought what a kind young man he was, not knowing that he was merely looking after his own interests. Darren always had an eye to the main chance; unusual in such a young man. When he had been left a considerable sum of money by his Grandfather, he didn't dash off on holiday or buy a fast car, he bought two of the terraced houses, one for himself at the end of the road and one to let out in the middle of the street. Almost at the same time his Uncle William had retired from his job at the foundry which had provided a tied house, and Darren found himself with the ideal tenants. Nora and William kept the house in perfect order, and Darren had not a moment's worry about them.

Nora carried all the ironing upstairs closely followed by Dodi. Dodi always seemed to be able to wake up the moment that Nora left the room despite not being able to hear anything; he had a 'sixth sense' about these things. Dodi plodded up the stairs, at Nora's heels, into the spare room where the airing cupboard was and waited while she packed away the sheets and pillow cases and then followed her into her bedroom where her clothes were kept. The ironing smelled warm and fresh and reminded Dodi of sleeping on the rose-patterned duvet cover that Nora liked best. When everything was carefully put away they returned downstairs, Nora holding the stair-rail and Dodi bouncing cautiously from one step to the next as if he was counting them in his head. Nora knew that he didn't like coming down the stairs so she always went especially slowly. At the bottom he looked up at Nora to see where she was going next ready to follow her lead.

Nora intended to make herself a cup of tea and a sandwich for lunch, she might have a piece of the new fruit cake she had made too and watch 'Bargain Hunt' on TV, her favourite programme, with that nice gentleman Tim Wannacott who always looked so smart. She didn't watch 'Bargain Hunt' every day, but liked a bit of a mid week treat. She went into the kitchen and noticed the coins on the side so first she loaded them into the meter – that would last a while she thought.

It was a warm day so the back door was slightly ajar letting a cooling breeze into the kitchen and allowing Dodi to come and go outside whenever he wanted to. The back door had a Yale lock as it was the most used door and right next to the alley gateway. There was no step to the garden which was completely fenced so he couldn't come to any harm. There didn't seem to be any cats that used the garden any more so he was quite safe from those horrors. There was a big water bowl outside for him which was usually kept full with rain water but occasionally Nora would check it and fill it up to the brim so that it was always there for him. He seemed to drink lots of water all the time. The smaller bowl in the kitchen was kept full too, although that needed filling much more regularly. Nora glanced out at the garden bowl, that was full, and the kitchen one was too. She began to make her lunch. Dodi watched her, he usually got a small snack at lunch time too and he looked forward to that.

Nora reached down into the side cupboard for his treats, the catch didn't click very well on the cupboard door and it was always springing open. Dodi was very good though he never tried to get his own snack even though he could easily have done so by nudging the packet on the shelf so that it fell over on its side spilling the little bone shaped biscuits out for him to pick up. She noticed that the box was half full; she would need to pick up another one next time she was at the Co-op.

Dodi and Nora walked into the sitting room and she switched on the television, it took a moment to flicker into life and then there was Tim talking to the contestants about why they were there and what they hoped to buy. Nora felt suddenly very tired, she put down her tray on the side table and plumped up the cushions, she took a sip of her tea and passed one of his treats to Dodi. It was William who had discovered the little bone biscuits in the pet shop and they had remained Dodi's favourites. She did miss William, she thought about him everyday, they had been inseparable since they had retired, talking about this and that, going to the shops and on their outings with Dodi. William appeared in her mind's eye and she had the feeling that if she looked towards the doorway he would be there smiling at her. She shook her head and concentrated on the TV, *'it doesn't do to get morbid'* she thought.

She reached for her sandwich and took a bite, perhaps she had done a bit too much ironing or whizzed the Hoover around too fast, she certainly felt very weird, slightly fuzzy in her head and a bit clammy like you feel when you are going to be sick. Suddenly she felt a sharp pain in her chest, it made her fall forwards and she dropped the sandwich on the floor. Dodi sniffed at the sandwich thinking it was something she had given him, but it was cheese and not one of his favourites, he was puzzled that she had dropped it for him. Nora was gasping for breath and Dodi sensed something was wrong; he began to lick her hand and then her face, since it had suddenly become so close to him. He sat up in a begging position and gave a little cry to her, he got down again and walked around to her other side, she was clutching her chest and panting like a dog – Dodi reached up and put his front paws on her knees to see her face better but she didn't seem to be able to move properly and didn't reach down to him to muzzle the top of his head; Dodi was completely confused. Nora was not behaving properly, he couldn't understand why she was not eating her sandwich, she never gave it to him, he always had his own treats, some of which were still there on her plate. He went over to the little table and reached up to the plate to see if he could get one for himself, he knocked the plate so the other part of the sandwich and his treats fell to the floor. Nora didn't seem to notice, all those crumbs on the floor too, he snuffled them up quickly and then turned to look at her again, something was very wrong, Nora wasn't touching him like she usually did and her hand was twitching strangely. He barked at her questioningly but nothing happened.

Suddenly the twitching stopped. Dodi lay down beside Nora's chair and slept, he hoped that when he woke up everything would be ok again. When he awoke it was dark outside, the afternoon had gone and still Nora was doubled up in her chair with her hands flopped over her knees and they were very, very cold, he licked them to warm them but they stayed cold – her eyes were open but they were not looking at him. The TV was still playing to itself and the lamps were still on so the room seemed almost normal.

Dodi wandered out into the kitchen and through the open door into the garden for a wee. When he came back he had a drink from his kitchen bowl and wondered when Nora would wake up to get him his dinner, he plodded into the sitting room and decided to try the sandwich since she didn't seem to want it, the cheese was hard and chewy but quite nice and he found another one of his treats which had slid under the side of the chair. He felt quite full now so he lay down next to the chair with his head on his paws looking at Nora, in a moment or two he was asleep and snoring loudly. This time Nora didn't nudge him to be quiet and he slept on undisturbed.

Chapter 2: Mary

Mary had been pleased when William and Nora had moved into the house across the alley, the house had been empty for a while and it was uncomfortable to have empty property so close, suppose a family of squatters moved in, or people started dumping stuff in the garden, she would hate that. When William and Nora first introduced themselves she had been delighted, people of her own age and clearly quite comfortably off. Under Nora's ministrations the house took on a shine it hadn't had before and she and William often sat in the small garden to have a cup of tea and invited Mary to join them if she wasn't busy – it was a real comfort to have them there.

Why on earth had they decided to get a dog when they retired? It had spoiled things a bit. Mary wasn't keen on dogs, the smell of them made her cough. She could see that this little one was quite cute, but he was so demanding of their time, they were always taking him out with them and he was constantly bouncing around them in the garden. They didn't seem to mind him running about and barking when he wanted something, but it annoyed her. She supposed that probably she was a bit selfish about it, she had hoped they would be able to do things together when they had first moved there, not expecting to take second place to a dog. They did everything with that dog, he went everywhere with them seemingly. People and pets!

When William became ill, Mary had helped Nora a lot, and so had the girl on the other side of her, collecting shopping, or prescriptions or just sitting with William when Nora had to go out, but the dog had been there all the time, watching her and not moving from William's side. They even allowed it to lay on the bed next to them or at their feet – ugh the smell!

Mary was sorry for Nora when William died, and did understand that she would at least have some company from the dog. They had both loved the little dog and Mary guessed that Nora would now draw a lot of comfort from knowing that William had shared him right from the beginning of their time with him.

Mary expected to see a bit more of Nora when she was a widow like herself, but it hadn't really worked out like that. They kept to their pledge to call on one another during the week, and to look out for each other. They organised a little scheme, if Mary's front door curtain was still pulled across at 11am, then there was something wrong and Nora should call. If Nora's back door was still open at 6pm then Mary should call on her to check that everything was ok. Often the door was still open at 6pm because Nora had left it open for the dog and forgotten to shut it, after a while Mary stopped bothering about the door, and just called once or twice a week for a chat and a cuppa. It seemed enough.

On Wednesday Mary heard the dog bark more than usual but thought he was only playing as he usually did with a raggy toy that Nora would throw for him. Mary had seen him do this often, the raggy thing would be tossed in the air and he would go scampering off to find it and get really excited about it, occasionally barking with joy. When he brought it back he would roll on his back and kick his legs in the air, woofing and tossing his head and ears about making Nora laugh. Mary just watched these antics but never joined in the laughter. Today Mary went upstairs and glanced across at Nora's house, the kitchen light was on, the door was ajar as usual, Nora would no doubt be watching some TV programme and had forgotten to feed the dog. She waited a little while, the dog stopped barking – all was well.

On Thursday Mary went out for the day with her daughter who came to collect her in the smart car she drove these days since her marriage to the local bookmaker. Mary was very proud of Michelle and had often told William and Nora how well she had done since taking the apprenticeship at Hills bookmakers when she left school, and then marrying the boss! Nora and William had listened politely as they always did, but without children of their own how could they possibly know what parental pride felt like. *'I suppose the dog was as close as they got to having a child to look after'*, Mary mused. She wondered how old it was now, probably about 10 or 12 years she supposed, *'little dogs didn't live very long did they, so she would get Nora back when it died'*, she thought - unkindly.

Mary and her daughter went to Ripon for the day – nice shops and a lovely lunch and then Michelle surprised her by suggesting that she came and stayed with her for a couple of days, they would go back to Mary's house, pack a few things and then have dinner at Michelle's house with her husband and his mother. Mary was thrilled, she had only been to the big house once before but it was so luxurious and a real treat. She wondered secretly if Michelle had something special to tell her, they had been married for over a year after all and David wasn't that old!

When they arrived back at her house Mary rushed up to her room and put some clothes into an overnight bag, she was so excited by this unexpected little 'holiday' that she forgot to look to see if Nora's door was still ajar. The dog wasn't barking that was a blessing, although it might have reminded her to look across at her old friend if it had been. Blissfully unaware of anything happening elsewhere, Mary concentrated on getting things together for her break. She remembered that it was her birthday tomorrow and realised why Michelle had planned this little excursion for her with the surprise at the end. Mary didn't bother much with birthdays now she was over 70; just another day. William and Nora had always celebrated them and had indeed invited her for a meal a couple of times for one or other of their 'special days' as they liked to call them. That wasn't an idea she subscribed to for her birthdays, too expensive by half.

Michelle drove the silver Mercedes confidently and Mary was pleased to notice that the lad at the end of the road, Darren, was out in his garden as they went past in the smart car. Michelle had been quite interested in him when they were at school together, thankfully that had blown over once she got to work. He was a nice enough lad, but was never going to make anything of himself, he worked in the garage as a mechanic and also seemed to have a few odd jobs, mostly for Nora and William window cleaning, grass cutting and the like. Nora was his Aunty so that was nice of him she supposed; but Michelle was aiming much higher than that and had caught the eye of the boss as Mary had intended. Nora had been surprised when Mary had told her about that, wondering if the 30 year age gap might be a bit much but Mary had assured her that David was kindness itself and would look after her girl really well. *'Older men are much more attentive'* she assured Nora. She thought that perhaps Nora had been keen that Darren settled down with Michelle, and she was pleased that hadn't gone any further.

As it happened, Mary stayed for four days with Michelle, yes there had been a 'something special' to tell and they were all thrilled about it. Mary couldn't wait to tell Nora that she was going to be a grandma; how jealous Nora would be!

When she got back, Michelle came in with her to bring her bags. Michelle was a kindly girl often a bit more thoughtful than Mary was herself, she said *'Mum don't go over the top telling Nora about all this, she doesn't have children herself and might be quite upset to be reminded that she won't ever be a grandma like you. Maybe you shouldn't tell her just yet, work up to it gradually. Perhaps I will come over soon and tell her myself, it might be easier for her if I do it, won't sound like you showing off, know what I mean?'* Mary agreed, Michelle was so much more careful of people's feelings, she wished sometimes she could be more like that herself, but she had always waded straight in and then thought about it later. Usually when she saw people's hurt faces she ticked herself off with *'Why did I have to say that?!'*

She decided she would go and see Nora tomorrow, Monday, much better than barging in on a Sunday – they never visited each other on a Sunday so Nora would guess something was different and then she would end up blurting stuff out as Michelle had known she would. No she was right, leave it a bit, let Michelle do it in her own way, she had always had a soft spot for Nora and William, treating them as an extra aunty and uncle when she was younger. And then there was that thing with Darren, Nora's nephew. Yes better to leave it to Michelle, and somehow there was quite a lot of joy in having such a secret anyway.

On Monday Mary noticed the back door was ajar as usual and the TV or radio was on, the curtains were pulled open so Nora was obviously up, she was just about to open her gate to go across the alley when the dog gave that annoying bark that said he wanted something. Nora and William had seemed to understand everything he wanted and could fulfil his wish as soon as he gave a single bark, but she still found it really annoying to see Nora dominated by the little dog. She could not understand why Nora was so compliant; it was after all 'only a dog'. Michelle's words came back to her and she realised how true they had been. Nora and William only had the dog and each other, no children; now Nora only had the dog, of course she would give in to it. *'I shouldn't be so mean spirited',* she thought and went back indoors.

Mary decided to do her shopping first and then pop into Nora's on her way home. Monday was a particularly busy day in town, everywhere was crowded, there were long queues waiting to pay and the weekly shop took ages. By the time she got back on the bus she had no energy left to do anything but get into her front door, unpack the shopping and make herself a welcome cup of tea; she would go to Nora and have a nice long chat tomorrow. After all they weren't in each other's pockets. Nora would understand that she had been really busy, they were good friends. While she was drinking her tea, the dog gave another sharp bark or two and then all was quiet. Surely he would bark his head off if anything was wrong.

Michelle rang on Tuesday morning and they had a nice long talk, Michelle said she would be over on Wednesday so would go and tell Nora her news then. Mary got on with her washing and wondered why Nora hadn't popped in to see her, perhaps she was busy too. She knew she couldn't keep the secret if she went into Nora's now, so she decided to wait until Michelle came on Wednesday morning. They would both go in together. How exciting it would be to talk about the baby.

Chapter 3: Darren & Paula

Darren had been mediocre at school. He liked it well enough, he could cope with the work but it always seemed so pointless somehow. He was a practical lad, his Dad had worked with William at the foundry and Darren had been apprenticed for a while to a local engineer, he had enjoyed the work and been content to move up to second in command after a few years. The boss and he shared the work and Darren found that he was competent with machinery and got a lot of satisfaction from taking something in that was broken and making it work. The garage wasn't too busy, enough to keep them both going and he brought home a reasonable wage. When his Dad died suddenly of a heart attack he was left to care for his mother, which he also did very competently. William helped him when he could but was not really surprised when Darren's Mum suddenly announced that she would be leaving to live with someone she had met at a dance. Darren's Mum had always been what William called 'flighty'. Darren had never really felt close to anyone, he was a bit of a loner, so the loss of his Mum just meant he had a bit more time for himself and no-one to pester him to go to the shops or put more money in the pot.

Darren had not realised quite how well off his Granddad was until he died. Darren's Granddad had watched the lad being an apprentice, looking after his Mum and felt proud of how he had coped.

He had no-one else to leave his money to, so he left it all to Darren. It was quite a shock when the solicitor told him after the funeral. The family solicitor knew Darren's Mum, he knew too that Darren would be too soft with her if she learned of his good fortune; so he had promised the Grandfather that he would look after the boy's interests. Luckily because he was the only beneficiary, he was the only one who had been summoned by the solicitor, so his mother had not even needed to hear about the will. On the same day that he told Darren about the legacy he also told him about the two properties for sale on Rydal Street. He advised him that it would be an excellent source of income if he lived in one and let the other and it would ensure that his legacy remained intact for the future. Darren liked the idea a lot, he hated the council house he had lived in with his mother and now he was stuck in a cupboard called a one bedroom flat. *'Yes'*, he thought, *'a little terraced house would be nice.'* He promised to look at the properties as quickly as possible, and within a week or two with the help of the kindly solicitor, they were his.

William and Nora had been at the Grandfather's funeral, they were also in a council house on the other side of town, but it was really too big for them and they told Darren that they were hoping to move, maybe swap to a smaller place on another estate. Darren quickly realised that this would solve his problem – how to obtain good tenants for his other property. The arrangement was quickly made; it was a perfect solution for everyone. Darren promised to make regular visits to keep up the maintenance and cut the grass for them if they wanted him to, for which they were very grateful, especially when it became too much for William. Darren was conscientious about his visits, and he thought they even looked forward to them.

To be fair he didn't know them terribly well, his family weren't the close type although they were his Aunt and Uncle, but they seemed a nice old couple and it felt quite good to be helping someone in the family. The rent was always paid on time and they hardly ever asked him for anything, the grass cutting allowed him to keep an eye on his property without being obvious about it, although he had only recently started that because William's sight had become too poor to allow him to be in charge of an electric mower. Aunty Nora was a housewife of the old fashioned sort; she had never touched an electric lawn mower. Darren usually remembered about the grass cutting on a Friday and it seemed a good day for it, end of the week but not the weekend, suited everyone really. Fridays after work became his regular slot during the summer months.

Darren appeared regularly at the bottom of Rydal Street, he had the property at the top and he occasionally called in on Nora on his way back from work. When he realised that his childhood girlfriend Michelle was the daughter of William and Nora's neighbour the visits became more frequent, but Michelle had changed a lot since she had left school and was more than a little distant with Darren for which he was quite sorry. He wasn't a lad with lots of girlfriends, Michelle had been a special friend, but now she seemed to be someone else's girl. She was still nice to him although her mother sneered at his *'little job in the garage',* not knowing of course of his inheritance. Then before he knew it Michelle was married to her boss, as her mother had intended.

Darren was standing in his garden on Thursday morning when Mary and Michelle drove by in the Mercedes, he noticed the car, cars interested him, but he barely noticed either the driver or the passenger, he had other things on his mind.

Darren was sorry when William died, he had liked the old man, he was good company. His Uncle and Aunt lavished a lot of love on the little dog Dodi they had got a few years ago and brought to the house, and Darren had quite liked it although it was a bit dominant. He couldn't imagine himself answering its every bark like William and Nora did. Darren had promised to visit more often when Nora was alone, but somehow he was always so tired at the end of a busy day at the garage and his visits quickly slumped to a weekly or fortnightly one to cut the grass in the summer and change light bulbs or clean the boiler in the winter. His Aunt Nora always made him a cuppa and usually had a freshly baked cake on the go. He loved the way they had made the little house so cosy and he tried to emulate that style in his own property, he was hoping that one day he would find someone to give it the 'woman's touch', a phrase his Aunt was fond of using; and he understood what she meant. You can get all the right furniture and bits and pieces but women had a way of putting things around that looked right and felt right, he just hadn't been able to do it. When he had first moved into his property he assembled all the things he thought he needed and then brought his Aunt round to 'organise' it. Within a few hours, with him fetching and carrying and her giving directions the house looked less like a warehouse and more like a home, he watched her do it but still wondered what the secret was.

His Aunt's house was spotless, he could certainly manage that and gradually he made his house feel like a home and was glad. Next door to his Aunt's house had been a family. Their cat had injured his Aunt's dog Dodi and shortly afterwards the family had moved away. Eventually a young woman had moved into the house, she was as the saying goes 'well fit'. He watched her leaving for work in the mornings, she had to walk past his house to get the bus into town, every day she looked so smart, not different clothes but different combinations of clothes. In winter she had a warm coat on top so that what she was wearing was less obvious, but in summer he could enjoy her summer tops and swinging skirts or thin trousers; she was lovely, and she appeared to be single. One day he was at his Aunt's house when she called to see if there was anything Nora wanted from the shops, he discovered that she worked in the chemist in town, she smiled shyly as she told him in answer to his question and he thought; no he *hoped* that it was because she was interested in him. The next time he went into town for his shopping he found he needed shampoo from the chemist and thus they had begun a light hearted but enjoyable friendship. They went to films or for a drink occasionally. Her name was Paula. Darren was hoping that his relationship with Paula would develop into something more – it was lovely to be friends but he hoped that she realised that he was ready to 'go serious'.

Darren decided to call on Nora on Friday this week, he had missed Friday last week because he had been away with Paula, and he felt guilty about it. But Paula had called him at work on that Friday morning and asked if he could meet her after work and take her to the station as her Dad was very ill and she had been asked to get to Preston as quickly as she could to see him. She was obviously upset and Darren completely forgot about his Aunt. He had dashed to the chemist as soon as his final job was done and they had shot off to the station. Paula was very upset and he could hardly let her travel alone at this difficult time, he had no ties and it was the weekend; so he got a ticket for himself and they journeyed down together. He was sure that not only would Nora understand, but she would be pleased for him that he had at last found someone who cared about him and wanted to be with him. He would probably stay in a hotel in Preston while Paula was with her family and then travel back with her the next day.

Paula's family made him very welcome; they had a large house and offered him a small attic room for his brief stay. When she saw how ill he was Paula wanted to be with her Dad for a long as she could, and it wouldn't be long the doctor suggested. Amid the sorrow in the family, Darren couldn't help feeling some small sense of joy that he and Paula seemed suddenly to be 'an item'. Over the weekend Paula's Dad worsened, he died on the Sunday with his family around him. Paula said she would have to stay with her family for a while longer but she expected and understood that Darren needed to go back to work. Darren rang his boss at home. Darren had become a perfect apprentice and subsequently a friend, his boss told him to take a few more days; things at the garage would be fine if he came back at the end of the week. This would allow him to help Paula sort out her Dad's affairs and would certainly bring them closer than ever. He told Paula he could stay with her until Wednesday, she was so grateful and flung her arms round his neck – *'I can't tell you what this means to me Darren to have you here with me now. I need to be strong for Mum, maybe I will bring her back with me when the funeral is over, but right now to have you here for a few days, it will make it so much easier, thank you, thank you for organising it, you are so much more than a friend.'* Darren glowed. Wouldn't Nora be pleased, he would tell her all about it when he called to cut the grass on Friday.

Darren helped Paula with all her arrangements and sometimes just sat and held her hand while she cried. She tried to put a brave face on things for her Mum, but needed to let out some emotion later with him. He felt wanted and loved and realised that maybe now his little house would soon get that 'woman's touch'. Darren travelled back early on Wednesday morning leaving Paula to attend the family funeral on the Friday and probably return with her mother on Sunday.

Darren felt duty bound to go into work on Wednesday afternoon as his boss had been so kind; even though he was dog tired. He worked late to make up some time and then was late home only finding a parking space at the end of the next road so that he had to walk a fair way carrying his overalls and steel-toe-capped boots. As he opened his gate he noticed a police car parked opposite the little lane between his aunt's house and her neighbour Mary's. *'Probably those little tykes in the house opposite, always in trouble, never with the police before now, but it was only a matter of time.'* He felt very tired suddenly, the time with Paula's family, the journey and the extra work had left him exhausted. He would have a cup of tea, make some dinner and have an early night. Probably go up to Nora's tomorrow evening after work, the grass would wait. He had so much to tell her but he was far too tired to begin that now. Nora would understand.

Chapter 4: Dodi – 'home alone'

Being a dog Dodi can only think with a limited visual vocabulary; dogs have a needs based response to situations, their main focus being on survival and to some extent comfort. Shih Tzu's are one of the oldest registered distinct breeds in the world, their 'style' dating back to the 16th century; they were temple guard dogs in Tibet.

What would it have been like for Dodi just prior to and then after Nora's death? How would he react to the situation that developed for him? Dogs probably have very little sense of time, there is day and night, meals, drinks and walks. Dogs love routine but only day and night continued to be part of Dodi's routine after Wednesday.

I like it here. This is my house. Him is gone, but Her is nice to me and she understands what I want. I can make Her do things when I bark or look. I don't like the stairs anymore, can't really see them coming down, but if Her is with me then I go the same stair as Her.

Nice to go outside, we don't go on so many trips now, just my garden smells now and sometimes a walk to the big grass.

No cat now, better in the garden.

I follow Her when she moves around the house, don't want to lose her, Her is my main friend, has the food, has the water, lets me out, throws my toy to play, takes me for little walks.

Wednesday:

We watch TV having lunch. I look at Her for my treats.

Hey! what is happening now, not right, not right.

Her makes a funny face, open and shut her mouth, I get up to her legs but Her won't stop opening her mouth, then Her stopped and went sleep. Get better when sleep, all animals get better when sleep.

Bread and rubbery (cheese) *fall from plate and my treats. Eat treats tried bread it ok – filled me up. Not so hungry now.*

Why is Her sleeping so long, never does that, always makes my dinner now. Her hands are cold, don't like the cold hands. Lick them warm, not warm up.

Night time not in bed, why not in bed? I must stay here with Her so she knows where I am when she wakes up. Is Her hibernating animal, never done it before?

Eat all my little biscuits in my bowl, not as good as dinner but good. Tummy warm and full. No biscuits left in bowl.

Thursday:

Her never moves now. We stay here all day. I barked for my dinner but no dinner. Now it's dark outside, I go for my water but I don't want to go out alone in the garden dark so I drink from the kitchen bowl. I hope Her will wake up for my breakfast.

I lick Her hand again, but it stays cold. I will lay here with Her today till she wakes up.

Sunshine is warm, Her likes sunshine but not waking up. I go in the garden to wee and drink. Not supposed to do toilet in garden but Her not taking me out so I have to. Very hungry now, will get biscuits from my cupboard, knock the box. Not many biscuits left.

Her cupboard has other biscuits in long packets, hard to break. Cut my mouth on the packet but the biscuits are big and nice. Not so hungry now.

Friday:

Found vegetables, big orange hards (carrots), *big brown hards* (potatoes) *and green softs* (cabbage). *Can only bite small bits of the hards, don't like the brown hards makes me feel sick. Ate the greens a little bit. Tried more big biscuits, lots of crumbs on the floor.*

Her still not waking. Give a bark to wake Her, no moving. Go out to sniff and wee, give a bark to come in, then push the door. Mouth hurts from cut and front teeth are wobbly, stops me from tearing packets, teeth hurt lots. One packet had cleaning sponge in, she uses them for floor if I drip my water - it is not all food in Her cupboard.

Found a packet with small white food – tasted funny and hard – once had these little stones (rice) *from Him but not the same as this, it was, soft, hot and nice.*

Bark for my dinner, not sure if it is dinner time or breakfast. Her not move, bark again and again. Tired now – sleep with Her again.

Saturday:

Got into the cupboard to find more packets. No more packets with food smell. Kitchen bowl empty, have to go out to garden for drink now.

Little white stones make me drink more, garden bowl nearly empty. Rain will fill it. Rain is cold, no towel to dry me. Sleeping more now, not so hungry when asleep. Her still hibernating.

Under the sink a cold tap pipe is slightly leaking water, it makes a small puddle on the shelf which

Dodi finds, he clears the puddle and then looks around the cupboard for more food.

In cupboard found drips to lick.

Sunday:

The TV is still on it is bright and white at night, shows me where Her is sitting, but not moving. Don't touch hand now, too cold, not hibernating – dead smell!

Who will help me? Bark - not too much, not right to bark too much in house or garden. Mary hates barking. Mary not coming to see Her. Darren not coming to see Her. Her sees no-one any more, not even me.

Monday:

Too tired to find more packets. Go to sleep now, go hibernate now.

Tummy hurts, lick my biscuit box, some crumbs on box, lick makes box soft but not good to eat. Find small meat boxes with silver paper on, spit out paper taste very strong meat, need more drinking. Have to go outside, no more rain in bowl, just a little to drink. Lick the grass some water there takes away the strong meat taste, eat some grass.

More teeth loose now and hurting. TV flickers and goes out, lights go out. TV gone now. Lights gone now. Seems cold and dark in house.

Tuesday:

Lots of days and nights have gone. No-one comes to Her. No-one comes to me. Wind made door slam shut, won't open to garden now, bark and bark, no-one comes. Have to wee and toilet on the floor, feels wrong, feels bad.

Sleeping in kitchen doorway, head on paws to watch Her. Too tired to look in more cupboards, no more biscuits, only orange hards. No more eating now I have to guard Her death sleep.

Wednesday:

No food anywhere only brown hards, can't eat those. Licked the pipe puddle in the cupboard, licked my bowl again. Feel sick, it's bad smell here, can't get to garden.

Big crashing, big big crashing at door makes floor moving, door breaks.
Run to her, stand next to chair. Growling, snarling, keep people away.
These are not Darren, not Mary, not Paula.
Bite their hands, bite their legs to guard her.
Too tired to jump, I want death sleep now, fall back down.

'Get off dog, get it out of the way Lucie!' The WPC picks up Dodi.

Soft hands pick me up hold me gently – it's ok, no more biting.

'Oh, you poor little thing, how long have you been here on guard? Sarge…I think he's deaf, he's not responding to any sound I make, he seems to have bad sight too, poor little chap, isn't it sad, he's like a skeleton, how long can he have been here?'

Chapter 5: The Police rescue

On Wednesday morning bright and early Michelle arrived for coffee with her Mum, but they were both so excited that they decided to pop into Nora's and have coffee with her. Mary went through the garden gate and noticed that the back door was now shut. What with everything that had happened, she had quite forgotten to look at the door from her upstairs window yesterday. They knocked on the door but now there was no sound from the house. Mary felt slightly guilty that she had not really noticed that the dog hadn't barked for a few days, now that fact leapt into her mind.

'Michelle, something's not right, usually the door is open and the little dog rushes out, I haven't heard him for a couple of days!'

'Oh! Mum, I hope Nora is ok. Perhaps she has just gone to the shops and we didn't notice, sometimes she takes Dodi with her doesn't she?'

'Not usually to the shops, she doesn't like leaving him tied up outside.'

'I'll go round the front and see if I can tell if she is in or not.'

Michelle was a very polite girl, she didn't really like looking through the curtains, but she was feeling a bit concerned now. She peered through the nets, with her face really close to the glass so that she could see a bit of the sitting room through the lace. Nora was in her chair in front of a blank TV, but she was slumped over with her head on her lap. The little dog was laying by her side. Michelle gasped as the full implication of what she was seeing hit her. She ran round to the back of the house.

'Don't you have a key Mum?'

'No, we never did that, exchange keys. Why what's wrong?'

'Maybe Darren has a key, I think Nora is ill, she is sitting very strangely in her chair and the TV is off. I'll run down to Darren, you wait here, or better still go back home till I come back.' Michelle didn't want her Mum to see Nora like that.

Darren of course wasn't in; he was still on the train from Preston. Michelle was so sure that things were not right that she decided to ring for the police as soon as she got back home. She arrived breathless and had to stand for a moment puffing and panting. Then she picked up her Mum's phone and dialled 999. The kindly girl she spoke to assured her that they would send a squad car round as soon as possible, but not to worry, usually in these cases, everything is ok and the old person has just dozed off. Michelle was sure that this would not be the case; no-one could sit like that for long.

The police car arrived about half an hour later, they had been on another call and came as soon as they could. Michelle explained and took them next door; she told them both doors were locked. Mary sat in her kitchen wondering why she hadn't gone over to Nora as soon as she got back, why did she leave it so long, why was she so selfish?, *'Poor Nora, please let her be ok. I'd even look after the dog while she is in hospital, it would make me feel better about myself'* she thought ruefully.

The police sergeant looked through the curtains, he was sure about what he saw and went back to the car for his battering ram. His colleague a young WPC called Lucie returned with him. He had seen the little dog and not being a great dog lover himself wanted someone else to deal with it. Before he started on the door, he asked Michelle if anyone else was a key-holder, she explained about Darren, Nora's nephew and also that she had tried him and he was out. She wasn't sure of the number of the garage where he worked.

The sergeant was a broad tall man and the ram took the door out at the first thrust. Michelle was about to rush in but he stopped her. The smell in the house was overpowering, he didn't want her to be the first to find the body in the state it would be in after several days; it was clear to him from the smell that it would have been several days. He wondered why the dog hadn't moved at the sound of the ram, perhaps it was dead too?

'How can this happen in this day and age Lucie?' He muttered to the WPC.

He asked Michelle to wait outside for a moment and took Lucie in with him. It's all part of the training this stuff, he mused. Lucie crept up to the body, it looked horrible, very cold and very still and a very strange colour, the dog suddenly looked up, gave a little jump and snarled at her, then it rushed at her legs snapping and biting. It looked really fierce and Lucie tried to fend it off, getting her hands bitten for her trouble. For such a small and frail looking thing it packed quite a punch on the teeth front! Lucie didn't want the dog to run out of the door so she shut it, leaving Michelle out in the hall. Once the door was shut the smell was awful, but the little dog seemed calmer. The sergeant asked her to get it out of the way so Lucie got herself behind it by getting out of its sight line and gently picked it up, the snarling and snapping stopped and it flopped in her arms.

Lucie sensed that it was relieved to have someone there at last. She held it gently and took it into the kitchen. There she found a different set of smells, an empty food and water bowl and the disarranged cupboards. She kept hold of the dog and filled the water bowl, there was no food, but that was probably all right since the vet might not advise feeding too soon if it had been starved. When she put it down near the bowl the little dog lapped gratefully at the water and then collapsed on the floor. Lucie knelt beside it. She talked to it gently but it was definitely deaf, it gazed up at her with poorly sighted eyes. One looked like a cataract and one looked very damaged.

'Little dog, I'm so sorry for your loss.'

The sergeant came to the kitchen door and looked down at Lucie dealing so competently with the dog, he was so grateful that she was there, dogs were not his favourite thing when he had to break into a house; he had had a few bites in his time which had put him off.

'Bring him out we need to get him to the vet, it looks as if he has been here alone for some time judging from the look of her, I doubt he'll make it, but I'm sure you want to try.' He said kindly.

The sergeant rang for an ambulance and then spoke to his station to alert the Detective Inspector. He went out into the hall to do it and spoke to Michelle, telling her to go home to her mother and they would come round and talk to them as soon as they had talked to the Detective Inspector, removed the body and made the house safe. Michelle asked what would happen to Dodi the little dog. The sergeant tried to be kind.

'I don't think the little dog has been fed for a week, he is very very frail, we will take him to the vet but I doubt he will make it. Don't worry too much about it, we will do the best we can for him.'

'But my Mother could look after it for a little while I'm sure.'

'We'll talk about it later. For now I need to wait for my Inspector, get the body removed as soon as we

can, get someone to identify the body either here or at the morgue, and secure the house.'

As the sergeant was speaking Darren appeared, looking shocked and weary, he had seen the police car as he walked home, and then as he wondered about it he saw the comings and goings were at his Aunt's house. Then he ran. He arrived puffing and panting and looked from the sergeant to Michelle and back again. He glanced at the WPC holding the little dog, it looked dead. It looked like a bag of bones.

'What's happened here, I've been away, where's my Aunt Nora?'

Michelle burst into tears and ran back home to her mother. Darren looked doubly confused; the sergeant put an arm round his shoulders.

'I'm sorry lad, your Aunt appears to have died in the past few days and we have only just found her, it's not a pretty sight but we need an identification, do you want to wait for the Inspector?'

Darren collapsed against the wall and the sergeant led him to a chair in the hallway. When he had recovered Darren agreed to identify his Aunt as soon as the Inspector arrived. They sat there together and Darren told the sergeant as much as he could about Nora that was relevant, including when he had last seen her. He felt so guilty that it should have been last Friday.

'Lad, life happens. Don't beat yourself up, you weren't to know.'

Next door, Michelle was being comforted by her mother once she had got out what was wrong. Mary was feeling terrible, how could she have left her friend for so long without checking on her. She had Michelle, Nora had no-one except Darren and he only came once a week, she should have been a better friend. None of this she said to Michelle who was broken hearted and didn't need to be reminded of Mary's lack of consideration, especially not in her condition. Oh dear! Now Nora would never know.

When the sergeant came in later to talk to them, his WPC was holding the little dog and Mary felt duty bound to offer to take it, she knew should show some compassion. The WPC said that once it had been seen by a vet then if it was ok she would bring it back for them to look after. Lucie knew that she would not do that, the neighbour did not seem like someone who could comfort or care for a dog in this state, it was the way she had wrinkled her nose as she said she would take it. The sergeant was already at the door of the car when she left the two stricken people. Darren was back at his home talking to the Detective Inspector and the ambulance was on the way to take the body to the pathologist. There was already a small crowd of neighbours at the gate. They looked suitably shocked when they saw the emaciated little dog in Lucie's arms.

'Lucie, you take the dog to the vet, I'll deal with the body removal when the ambulance arrives and get someone to secure the property. Come back and collect me when you can.'

The post-mortem would show that Nora had been dead for seven days. Mary might have helped Nora, if she had called on the day that it happened. She heard the dog bark more than usual, but the door was ajar although it was quite late for it to be so, the TV was on, the lights were on so she assumed that all was ok. Darren might have helped Dodi if he had indeed been able to visit on the first Friday after Nora's death. Paula had her own bereavement to deal with.

Chapter 6: Dodi finds love again

When Lucie explained to the vet, the veterinary nurse took the little dog gently from her arms and placed it in an 'overnight cage' in the back of the surgery where the animals who had or were about to have operations were kept. The nurse assured Lucie that they would tranquilise him and give him some sustenance through a drip overnight and see how he was in the morning. They didn't hold out much hope. They were all sure that this little chap had only just made it to his rescue and that death would be a blessed relief for him. Lucie toyed with the idea that she should agree to let them 'put him to sleep'. But he had been so plucky to last that long, it seemed a bad way to end it after all he had been through. Perhaps he would just give up and die overnight and then she wouldn't be the one making the decision. She thought about contacting that neighbour but she was absolutely sure that she would not want to pay towards this little dog's upkeep at the vet. Lucie agreed to pay for the treatment herself but the vet wouldn't hear of it.

'We can do this for him, no worries, let's see how he is tomorrow.'

The next morning she arrived at the vet expecting the worse but the veterinary nurse was all smiles.

'He's made it!' He hates being in the cage though, so what do you want to do with him now? We can keep him for a couple of days until he stabilises a bit more and is eating proper food if that would help.

His front teeth are really bad and he is also 'intact', so if he gets back some proper strength he might need to be neutered as well as have his front teeth removed during the operation. He is going to cost a bit to get back to full health, if it's even possible. I'm afraid we can't do all that for you without being paid.'

Lucie felt a bit daunted by this information. Maybe it would have been better if he had died overnight, perhaps he still might not make it. He was old for such a catalogue of operations. Who would take this on?

Lucie rang her sergeant and told him the news. She would have kept him herself but she lived in a 'NO PETS ALLOWED' flat.

'Sarge. I know someone who works for a dog rescue centre, shall I ring him?'

'Yeah, you can if you want.'

Lucie rang her contact. Martin and his wife had been running a sort of dog shelter for a while now, they were actually dog breeders but occasionally took in older dogs that needed to be re-homed for various reasons. Babies came along and the dog was jealous, people moved abroad and didn't want to take the dog, someone died and no-one in the family wanted the dog, that sort of thing. Martin was far less sure about this little chap though, he sounded as if he really needed some 24 hour a day care for a while. His wife Janey said they should try him and see how he got on.

Dodi left the vets after three days. The vet had been Dodi's second new friend, there was no charge. Lucie took him along to the shelter.

The ground floor of Martin and Janey's house was given over to dogs, mostly to puppies. When he opened the door to her, Lucie was first assailed by the doggie smell of the place and secondly by all the tiny bouncing puppies who rushed out to greet her. Dodi was still very frail and when she put him on the floor, the puppies fairly swamped him, he jumped back and snapped at them and they all retreated. Martin laughed. *'Still got some spirit left then.'* Lucie asked Martin if he would be able to give Dodi the extra attention he would need for a while and he assured her that he would try. He said she could visit whenever she wanted to. She knew that he was really kind and would do his best for the little dog and there was really nowhere else. He also suggested that he would put an advert on his website and see how he got on. He did warn her that it might be difficult to find someone who would take an older dog with disabilities.

The advert was placed with a small photo of Dodi's face. Dodi looked sad and lonely as well as puzzled and elderly. No-one offered a home in the first month of the advert.

> Dodi is a dog with special needs. Dodi was left alone when his elderly owner died. She was not found immediately. Dodi is totally deaf, he is partially sighted, he is about 13 years old. Dodi is looking for a caring home where his special needs can be accommodated. He needs a home with no small children or other dogs if possible.

As time went by, Dodi settled a bit into the routine of the centre. He learned to try to get to the food bowl first or the puppies would snaffle everything. He found eating a bit difficult because of his loose teeth, so he could not eat fast enough. Martin spent some time fending off the puppies so that Dodi could get a bit more of the food before they clambered in, but it was quite a task. Dodi got a little stronger but he was still painfully thin. He liked the puppies once he got used to their boisterousness, they were a happy little bunch but he was always hungry. He spent a lot of time asleep, it was easier.

Dodi had enough to do getting some food each day, when things got too much for him he nibbled his feet and licked his coat, he created some sore patches on his skin but the pain took his mind off being hungry and waiting for Nora to come and take him home; and for a moment or two stopped him scratching at his somewhat mangy coat. His skin was flaky and he had a number of bald patches where he had yanked bits of fur out with his licking. He was not a cuddly looking dog. Martin began to give up hope of getting him a proper home and resigned himself to Dodi living with them for the rest of his no doubt short life.

~

In Cumbria my husband and I had just been to see our friends in the next village, they had just got a little dog from a rescue centre in the midlands. She was a Shih Tzu, a lovely honey brown with silky fur and a very cute face with big shiny eyes. Dennis really liked her and when we got home he went on to the Internet to look up these lovely little dogs that he had not really been aware of before.

Back in Suffolk a few years ago we had owned a lovely brown and white collie and had been distraught when she died of old age, we missed her terribly but had decided not to get another dog. Pets give you love and pain in almost equal measure; we did not want to put ourselves through that again. Fate though has a way of ignoring such sentiments.

The years went by and we found themselves with two rather special cats, both of them given to us for different reasons. Sam and Tigga were Birman's, beautiful Siamese coloured cats but fluffy and cuddly and who absolutely loved people. Sam was a 'chocolate point' (deep brown face, ears, tail and socks) Tigga was a 'grey point' (grey where she was chocolate). They were much more like dogs really and once Dennis and I had moved to Cumbria with them, they liked nothing better that to go for walks with us on the fellside, running and playing and chasing rabbits till it was time to go home.

Serious walkers who came across the Pennines were very amused to see two 'posh cats' out for a walk with their owners! When it was time to go home, we called, they followed us and we all walked back together.

One strange day Sam went missing, she had been out hunting and not returned in the morning, this was not unusual. She was much the tougher of the two and an accomplished hunter. Tigga and Sam often went out hunting at night, returning in the early hours with Sam clutching some poor dead creature in her mouth. Between the chest of drawers and the wall of the bedroom Sam would dissect her 'meal' with a great deal of crunching and slavering, which often woke me up. Tigga would be looking on, waiting for his share. They resembled a lion pair, the male waiting for the female to finish and leave him something, with Sam it was usually some very small titbit that Tigga was left, the ears and the feet perhaps. All the innards were dissected neatly and neither of them touched those.

When Sam disappeared without trace I believed that she had gone feral. I think I just could not cope with the idea that I would never see her again. Dennis and I and the whole village looked for Sam, she was so distinctive, notices were put up, vets were called, rescue centres scoured but she had totally vanished; no little body was ever found. Tigga, the gentler of the two became number one cat. He hated hunting. After Sam had disappeared, he would not even go outside and looked terrified if he was put out there. The vet suggested that Sam had been taken by an animal, a buzzard, a badger, a pole cat, all of which were prevalent in the area. Because Tigga had seen it happen and run home he was now petrified of being left outside. It was a plausible idea, but I still hoped she was just feral.

As years went by gradually Tigga would creep out if I was gardening and if the sun was shining but would always return with me to the house when I went in. He never again walked with us or went out alone. He never again went out at night and we had to get him a large permanent litter tray. We agreed that we would never have another pet after him.

As Dennis was looking for Shih Tzu's on rescue websites I leaned across from my desk to look and there was the little picture of Dodi. That sad little face touched my heart and I couldn't get him out of my mind. I had spent most of my academic career working in a variety of ways with children and adults who had significant special needs including sensory impairment; here was a dog who clearly needed the expertise that I might have accumulated during this work.

There were a couple of serendipitous events that preceded and contributed to Dodi joining our household:

- We had been to stay with our French friends the summer before and met their lovely new raggy dog called Dino. I had adored this dog right from the first meeting and really missed him when we got back. When I told my brother about him on the phone, he said *'Sounds like you're ready for another dog!'*

- A few months before our French friends arrived to stay with us, our National newspaper carried a double page spread seeking homes for dogs who had been in rescue centres for some time so were 'desperate for love'. One of these dogs 'Floyd' looked exactly like Dino (the French dog) and I wanted him. I rang the number given for Floyd and was answered by a young man. I told him I was a Doctor, I had owned a rescued dog before, didn't have a dog, I lived in the Cumbrian countryside and I was very interested in giving Floyd a home but as it was February and it would take me about seven hours of driving to get to Uxbridge, I might have to wait for better weather before I could get down to the south to collect him. I would though give them enough money to keep Floyd in comfort until I could get to him. This seemed to me to be a very reasonable offer for an older dog who had been in care for a while and who was 'desperate for love'.

The young man drew breath. *'Oh no, that's not how it works, you have to make three or four visits to meet a dog. We have to make visits to your home to check you out and then if we are satisfied we will let you take the dog*

> *away. You live too far away for this to work so I'm sorry, we can't put you on our list. Floyd has had 40 phone calls so far.'* I felt that my offer of unconditional love had been totally rejected. I hope Floyd found his loving home, I cut out his picture and I still keep it above my desk.

I kept looking at Dodi's picture on the Internet. He was definitely calling to me. I decided to wait until after our French friends had visited and then I would call. If Dodi was still available I would negotiate to have him. I had no idea that his little 'advert' had been on line for nearly a year.

Our friends left on the Friday. I asked my husband about Dodi. He was a bit reluctant, not least because of Tigga, but I assured him that as both of them were elderly I was certain that they would be fine together. I said this with fingers crossed behind my back. He was definitely unsure but said yes to please me. I rang the centre at 10am.

'This is Doctor Morgan, I'm enquiring about Dodi in your advert.'

Yes he was still available, and the gentleman I spoke to was amazed when he realised that I was offering to take him.

'Are you sure you want to take him, he's already old for a Shih Tzu.'

'I know we might not have him for long but we can give him a couple of good years of life.'

'He's totally deaf'

'Yes I understand'

'He's going to need some expensive veterinary work.'

'That's fine we have a good vet here, what is he like with cats?'

'I've no idea if he has ever met a cat.'

'Ok look, I am not interested in all this toing and froing that rescue centres seem to expect, If I drive down to you, it will take me about two and a half hours so if he likes me I want to be able to take him away.'

'Isn't it more if you like him?'

'No, he has to like me; I am bound to like him.' (I said confidently)

'Ok, we are just delighted that you are willing to take him on, but I have to take some precautions, could you bring some ID with you please Dr.Morgan.'

I set the SatNav and drove off towards Crewe. I arrived near to the centre by 12.30. I discovered that the road I wanted had been cut in half and I was at the wrong end of it. There was a fence at the end and when I got out of the car in disbelief I could see the other bit of the road ahead also with a fence at the end and a bit of 'no man's land' between the two. This was very confusing particularly to a satnav that was already calmly saying *'you have reached your destination.'* Luckily I had passed a bin lorry on the road parked up for lunch so I went back to it. The bin men explained carefully how to get where I wanted. It required a lot of left, left, left turns which I hoped I would remember once I got back into the town traffic.

'A lot of people get caught by it, don't really know why they did it, it's a right pain for us as you can imagine!' The bin men were a kindly crew, and carried on eating their sandwiches while I negotiated a twenty six point turn in the road in front of them!

I eventually found the other end of the road which led to a small council estate. There were older houses at the entrance to the estate, the sort that have settees in their front gardens and lads sitting on walls eyeing up the cars that go past with an obvious interest in what might be removable from them if they get parked up. My car would not be parked for long if I could manage it.

At the far end of the estate was a more modern set of houses and one of these was the rescue centre. A strong dog smell wafted around me as I went into the house and then what seemed like hundreds of tiny balls of fluff raced out to greet me, jumping up and making little tweeting noises. Martin introduced himself and then tucked the puppies away quickly – he clearly recognised how cute they were and didn't want their obvious cuddliness to detract from my meeting with Dodi. He went off to get him.

A painfully thin and bedraggled little black and yellow dog walked sedately into the room and looked up at me with semi sightless eyes, his fur was lank and greasy looking, it parted along his back and in some places touched the floor. He had a pathetic little spit of a tail and dangling black ears like fringes dragging on the ground. Two fangs and a lot of very jangly little teeth stuck out of his lower mouth. He was the ugliest dog I had ever seen in real life.

Who is this? Why is Her here?

I was totally shocked by how he looked – his Internet picture had done him more than justice. I bent down to pick him up. He smelled awful; Martin watched me. I was ready for a snarl or a snap, and I even found myself thinking, *'If he bites me I won't be able to take him.'* This was surprising since I have in the past been bitten by children and still carried on working with them; but this dog was *so* ugly, was he also vicious? I looked at Dodi, Dennis would be horrified by this dog I thought.

Her smells nice, Her knows how to hold me, is this my new person? Will Her have a rose quilt?

Martin said. *'I've tried my best to ensure that he gets enough food, but it's difficult with all the puppies, and sometimes I forget he's deaf and by the time he has got there the food is gone, I give him more of course but they are always at it. He will need things done to his teeth and I haven't managed to get his ears cleaned inside yet.'*

I was getting used to the smell while we talked. Martin was explaining what he knew of the circumstances surrounding Dodi's discovery. He suggested that Dodi might have been alone with his mistress' body for at least a week, but it was all a bit unclear. *'We were told that he was about 13'.* He said. I turned my head slightly and realised that Dodi had got his matted little arms round my neck and had laid his head on my shoulder and now he was sound asleep. How adorable is that! I thought *'I can't leave him here; he really needs to be properly looked after.'* Martin was looking at me hopefully,

'He sleeps a lot, it's all he seems to do really, but then he is old.'

'So is my cat', I said, *'If it's still ok, then I'll take him.'*

Martin really smiled then. I offered my passport and driving licence as ID but I think our conversation had convinced him that I was ok.

Will Her take me, will Her take me, please take me!

He helped me carry Dodi out to my car. I had no lead, no collar, no food, no bed. I had a blanket on the front seat and we put Dodi on it. He looked up at me as I got into the car ready for the drive back then he lay down on the blanket and slept until we got to Killington Services on the M6. I thought he might need a wee and then remembered that I had no lead or collar. I took off my belt, put it through the buckle once as a makeshift collar and then held the rest as a lead. I lifted Dodi out of the car and put him down in the car park. He sniffed at the nearest kerb stone and did a wee, then he just sat down and looked at me. He was *so* unappealing how on earth would I convince Dennis that we could love this dog!

On the way home I called into Appleby pet shop and bought a tartan collar and lead, a set of stainless steel bowls on a high stand, *(older dogs don't like to have to bend too low for their food),* some packets of dog food and mixer biscuits, and some tea tree shampoo. The pet shop owners are an elderly couple who have always been so kind to me when I have been in buying things for the cats. They were also very comforting when Sam disappeared and always asked about Tigga. I explained about this little smelly dog and they were so genuinely interested in him.

' Poor little thing, still if anyone can do it, you can.' I'm not sure how they knew this but their confidence spurred me on. They stroked him even though he was actually tacky and offered him a little bone

shaped biscuit which bless him, he tried hard to eat. It seemed as if he was already doing his best to fit in, he looked up at me all the time almost as if he was waiting to see what I wanted him to do next and whatever it was he would do it as best as he could.

I called into the vet, The veterinary nurse gave him a quick look to make sure that I wasn't taking any nasties into the house. I bought some Frontline (mites and fleas) and made an appointment for us to see the vet the following day for a proper estimate of the work needed. Then I went home. Dennis was out.

I got Dodi out of the car, and he immediately ducked down under the gate and was on the road outside our house! I put him back in the car, got some chicken wire out of the garage and made a spur-of-the-moment gate shield to protect him from the odd car and flock of sheep that he might encounter if he was on the road. He barked in the car, probably because he couldn't see me while I was fixing the wire. It was then that I realised the full significance of his deafness; that if he did get out I could not call him back, or look for him in the village calling his name. I had to know where he was all the time. He seems to realise this as well because he never lets us out of his sight either unless he is asleep!

I knew that the first thing I needed to do was to bath him, however messy it would be it had to be done; hopefully before Dennis got back. I took Dodi into the bathroom where we have a deep Victorian roll top bath; I hoped he wouldn't struggle too much, he seemed so frail. He stood in the bath completely still and waited – I was amazed. I gently put on the soap and worked up a lather, he just stood. With his fur wet his bones stood out, he was skeletal. I rinsed him off carefully and stood him on a warm towel, and still he just stood there looking at me. I gently rubbed him dry and only when he was dry did he try to shake himself. He was and continues to be amazingly easy to bath.

Dennis returned and I introduced them. Dodi looked up, Dennis looked down. I could see that he was struggling for something positive to say.

'Is he the same breed as Tia (our friends new Shih Tzu)?'

This was a kind way of saying that he looked nothing like her, she at least looked healthy and her coat was shiny and soft. Dodi continued to look up at Dennis and then he gave the tiniest wag of his tail and Dennis was captured!

'Poor little thing, we need to give him some love.' I was so grateful for his compassion.

Now I have a new Him, I like it here.

When Dodi was dry I put his lead on and took him out of the gate and towards the fellside. I realised that I was quite looking forward to walking a dog again. Dodi staggered 20 yards from the gate to our garage forecourt and then lay down. I picked him up and took him home. So much for a dog to walk I thought.

> *The house is easy, all tidy like home but no stairs to climb. I walk into Her bedroom, look at bed, a rose quilt - my heart jumps for joy!*

Each day I walked him a little further, sometimes carrying him and letting him walk back home. He had a good sense of where his gate was. The neighbours came to meet him. We are a very close community in this tiny village, a lot like a big family so everyone was interested in him. I could see in their faces that they all thought he was ugly and mangy and they felt very sorry for him. I could also see that they thought I had taken on a lost cause.

'Cor, that's a face only a mother could love!'

The vet suggested that Dodi would need an operation to remove the jangly teeth, they were hurting him and stopping him eating. It was imperative that this was done as soon as possible but not until he had put on some muscle and increased his general body tone. During the anaesthetic for the tooth operation she would clean out his ears and castrate him. Although she would not normally advise castration of such an old dog, since he was having an anaesthetic anyway it would be worth doing at the same time. She told me that one eye was damaged and one had a cataract, the damaged one was still healing but would probably only give peripheral vision, the cataract could only get worse. He weighed less than 3kg. We booked the operation date for a month later, during which time I had to try to increase his weight so that he had some substance to withstand the trauma of the operation. He had to have luminous eye-drops twice a day and ear cleaning drops. The eye-drops were not easy to administer as I dropped it on he shook his head the kitchen and I were covered in luminous greeny yellow gel, only a tiny portion remained on his eye, it didn't add anything to his look, but it did work. The ear drops were virtually impossible after the first attempt; he did not like anyone touching his ears so they would have to wait for the operation. Dog ear wax has an incredibly pungent smell.

I bought high protein food in tiny biscuit form, quality tinned dog food and accepted that he would have some of our food too, I would try to ensure that this mixture stayed within recommended quantities, not that the human food was an extra to the quantity of food he consumed. At first he ate everything that was put in front of him, including vegetables and cake, bread and toast. He seemed to be permanently ravenous. He did not though like quality dog food, his preference was co-op dog food which he had clearly had before. Gradually he bulked up so that by the time of his operation he weighed just over 5kg and the vet said it would be ok to try to sort out his problems now. She was actually not sure if he would make it through the anaesthetic but felt he deserved a chance; he would never get any better without sorting out his teeth.

He was at the vet's all day, I couldn't concentrate on anything, and I already missed him so much. When I went to collect him back he looked so pathetic, but he managed to wag his tail when I touched him. His mouth was flat now, no protruding jangly teeth, no fangs showing, just his little sore lips. The vet suggested that he wore a 'doughnut' collar to stop him licking his castration wound. She had, she said '*got a table load of muck out of his ears.*' He was almost certainly stone deaf but at least his ears would not now be sore and he would probably stop continually shaking his head. He smelled a lot sweeter too.

At home we placed him gently in his tweed bed and wrapped him in one of my jumpers as he was shivering from the operation trauma. I put the doughnut collar on him and he just hung his head looking for all the world like a Ku Klux Klan victim. I took it off. That first night after the operation I lay him in his bed next to my side of our bed and held on to his collar through the night to stop him licking his wound. The next day with a semi-numb arm I went into town to a charity shop to see if I could buy a babygro. The kindly shop lady saw me looking at the baby clothes and asked,

'How old is the baby?'

Not really concentrating, I said *'13'.* And then realised what she would think, and followed up with,

'Sorry, it's for a dog who has had an operation.'

'I'll leave you to look then.'

I cut out the sleeves of the blue striped babygro and fastened it on to him back to front, with the little pop studs along his back, and so that his scar was covered at night. He accepted it because he seemed to accept anything I did to him or for him. He still lay next to me so I could be aware of what he was doing, and once the scar began to heal properly it obviously itched a bit, but the little stripy suit did its job and the wound healed properly.

As his lips healed up his face took on a more cuddly look, he has a proper little mouth more like a human mouth than a dog and because his face is flat without the pointed nose of a dog he looks more like a teddy bear. As he put on weight, his legs got chunkier and he started to look really cuddly. Everyone in the village knew his story and once he began to look really cute the shocked looks disappeared. We took him on an outing to Grizdale Forest and a little girl said *'Look Mummy a little teddybear dog, I wish we could have him.'* Only a few months ago, no-one wanted him, now even children thought he was cute and cuddly. I felt proud of his pluckiness.

One day I took some things to the charity shop in town Dodi in tow on the lead. As it wasn't a food shop and I had my hands full I didn't pick him up. At the entrance to the shop was a basket containing small fluffy toys. Dodi looked at it and before I could stop him he had picked up a black and white dog (looking a bit like a small version of himself) and carried it comfortably in his mouth. I paid for the 'bear' and we took it home. He had not been at all interested in playing ball or tugging things but with 'bear' it was different. By throwing it along his eye-line he could see it and chase it. He always wants to play 'bears' after his dinner. He gets very excited when we pick up bear from his bed, we throw it for him several times, each time he brings it back to his bed and on the final run he lays in the bed and sucks at its hands and nose, the sucking makes him gradually fall asleep hugging his bear. It's very endearing.

Found a raggy again, every day this is more and more home.

Our friends in the next village found a dog groomer for their Shih Tzu and I made an appointment to take Dodi. Before hand I bought a set of electric dog clippers and gave him a little bit of a trim, mainly so that he would not be frightened when it was done properly. Each time I used them he was better at accepting the 'treatment'. I also found a picture of an adult Shih Tzu with a 'puppy cut'; rather than the long dangling coat that the show dogs have with silly looking ribbons in their top-knots. The puppy look was just right for him and the groomer was sure that she could achieve it.

I had made up my mind that if she was at all casual about him when I took him, then I would not leave him. He was by now attached to me as his carer and hated me to be out of his sight. She took one look at him and picked him up. While I was telling her his story and detailing bits of him that she needed to be careful with, I noticed that he had put his arms round her neck and laid his head on her shoulder. He had never done this with anyone else apart from me before. I felt confident to leave him.

When I returned he looked like a little bouncy puppy and his skimpy fur was glossy and soft. She had left more fur on his hips since they were so bony and thin and had done her best with his flaky skin. There was a way to go but he was certainly getting there. Dennis was delighted with how he looked. He was beginning to love him too.

The bad skin worried me a lot, he kept chewing at it and it had begun to look like eczema. I wondered if dogs got eczema and looked it up on the Internet. Apart from the detailed and horrific explanations and pictures, there was an advert for a herbal preparation to be mixed with food, it seemed worth a sample. Within a week of using it Dodi's skin had begun to heal up and he was no longer scratching and chewing at his legs and feet. I bought another month's supply and also told the groomer about it, she bought some for her dog and has found it equally good. Two other people in the village tried it with success. We now place a regular shared order.

When I first brought Dodi home, his eyes were weeping and gungy. Apart from the eye drops I bathed them every day with warm water and then with baby wipes. Gradually they started to brighten, the damaged one healed as much as it could but the cataract will not change. His eyesight is gradually worsening and I have to be his eyes on our walks, watching out for steps, holes in the ground and paths on steep slopes. I have to be wary of fence posts and ice; in effect my holding the lead is like holding his hand. I have to listen for cars and other threats. He has a harness rather than a collar now as it seems to feel more secure to him and less jerky than something pulling on his neck. I am his eyes and ears and he has absolute trust.

When Tigga first met Dodi, he just looked at him and walked away. Tigga has always been quite comfortable with dogs, he came to us from London and had clearly learned to stand up for himself there. The village dogs were quite frightened by a big white fluffy cat who walked towards them rather than ran away from them. Sheep dogs would cross the road rather than walk past Tigga's gate. So a small Shih Tzu was hardly a problem to him. He lived high for a day just while he was checking him out and then everything was back to normal. Dodi never barked at him, or ran at him or tried to eat his food. In the early days he would sometimes sit next to Tigga eating and wait to see if he would leave him anything and occasionally Tigga would walk away with a scrap left in the bowl, but at no time did Dodi attempt to muscle in on the bowl until Tigga had left it.

Tigga was Dennis's favourite, they had a 'special relationship'. When Tigga became fifteen he developed a number of difficult medical conditions that made his life unbearable to him and to us having to watch his painful decline. The time came when we had to make the decision for him; we had had Dodi about eighteen months by then and they were becoming good friends, sleeping together sometimes, laying in front of the fire together so it was doubly sad to think that they would have to be parted. Dennis was distraught at Tigga's imminent death, but by then Dodi had become a much loved and adorable pet and it certainly helped us both deal with our pain at Tigga's loss. The vet suggested that Dodi stay in the room *(she came to the house for the dreaded deed)* so that he would know that Tigga had gone. He did look for him occasionally in the following week but seemed to accept the loss better than I have known other animals do in a similar situation but who were not present at the end, so she was clearly right.

Dodi has now inveigled himself into Dennis's hard won affections. Dodi is now 'top man'. After Tigga's death, he took over the role of climbing onto Dennis's lap when he was reading the paper; Tigga had always done this, Dodi had never done it until Tigga was gone. Dennis is enchanted with this action. When Dennis goes swimming to the nearby spa he has a bacon roll for lunch, he always saves bacon for Dodi and Dodi watches for it as soon as he returns. Dodi can sit up perfectly like a storybook dog and when he does that he is irresistible. He only begs to us when we are alone never to guests and never if guests are at the table, he is so well mannered.

Him is nice, picks me up and cuddles me and brings me bacon when he goes out, love bacon!

We have turned Dodi's sad recent life into one of total joy. He has coats, fleeces and jumpers with harnesses to wear out on his walks and gradually he has learned to walk further and further; now he can manage to walk halfway up the fell side with his friends the two collies belonging to a neighbour. They run off and then come back to check on him as he plods along. He has a jaunty rolling gait when he is on the road with his flowing plume tail held high and a real bounce to his step. His coat is now thick and soft and there is nowhere on his body where you can see his skin or his bones. He is completely social with all other dogs and all people he meets. He is in fact the easiest pet I have ever owned.

At a recent Skype session with relatives in Canada we held up Dodi for them to see.

'Oh, how handsome he is!' I was thrilled to bits.

When he was new to us, we left him in the house to go shopping and asked a neighbour to let him out at lunch time, we forgot to warn him about Dodi's deafness. If he was touched when he was asleep he would start and jump and unless it was me, he would snarl and maybe bite. The neighbour went into the house, Dodi was asleep on the sofa, he bent down to pick him up and got a pair of fangs in his arm for his trouble! Not wanting to stain the carpet he went home to wrap his arm and brought his daughter-in-law back with as she was 'good with dogs'. By this time Dodi had got off the sofa and was in 'defend the house' mode. He would not let them down the hall. He did not get his trip out to the garden for a wee until we came home. After that incident I made sure that I touched Dodi a lot, when he was awake and when he was asleep, he needed to feel confident that a touch was not a threat. Now he has no problem with being touched in any situation. The neighbour is still a little wary but the fang scars have faded now and he was pleased with the bottle of wine in compensation.

'That wine was really nice, let me know when you want me to look after Dodi again!'

Only on one other occasion, shortly after we got him, did he show aggression. Dennis put down a piece of sausage for him from the table and then realised that it was a bit big, so he bent to retrieve it to make it smaller. Dodi thought the food was being taken away and started snapping, snarling and growling really aggressively. I put on leather gauntlets and picked him up from behind. I put him in the porch and shut the door. I have never heard a dog cry in that way, it was just like a child. I left him for a few minutes so the message would get home – *aggression means separation from me.* Then I brought him back in for a cuddle and he has never done anything like it again.

Dodi now accepts everything we do with him, car journeys, walks, trips to see friends, grooming, visiting the vet, whatever. He is a well known little person in the community. When a neighbour started telling someone new to the village about him, they said:

'Oh we already know about Dodi, he's a legend!'

When we went to the vet for his 1st annual check up I knew we had done well when she said:

'That is a different dog!'

Dodi just wagged his tail and looked happily at both of us.

Found love again, her loves me lots and lots. Her is my person now.

As I write this Dodi is probably fifteen, although he now looks much younger than that. We know that one day (hopefully not too soon!) we will lose him. He is very fit and healthy now but he is old and we will take our responsibility for him seriously if we have to make that awful decision. He may of course be kind to us and die in his sleep, which will be hard but not as hard as making the decision. When that time comes we will know with absolute certainty that we have done the best for him and that he has had a lovely, lovely life with us. He enjoys everything we do and he wants to be part of everything, when the time comes that he can't do things because he is too ill then he would not want to bear it. I will hold him close, he will put his head on my shoulder and his arms round my neck and that is how we will stand until the anaesthetic that the vet administers takes effect and his life is over.

This dear little dog will stay forever in our hearts, the loveliest, happiest and easiest dog we ever owned. As my elderly neighbour who feeds Dodi sausages whenever he sees him, says to other people:

'This is Dodi, the luckiest dog in the world.'

Dodi's Contacts:

Hair & Hound -Dog Grooming
hair.hound@btinternet.com

Old Hall Veterinary Centre
www.oldhallvets.co.uk

Pets Pantry
Appleby in Westmorland

Bionic Biotic
pooch@poochandmutt.com

Coats & Jumpers
www.muddypaws.co.uk

Dog bed
www.addicare.co.uk

Favourite charity
www.pdsa.org.uk

Other friends
www.hillhousemorgan.com
www.redprojects.com

Redstone Books - www.redstonebooks.co.uk

Printing & Binding -www.cpibooks.co.uk

Acknowledgements

I wish to thank
Linda, my talented and super fast proof reader who makes such good suggestions as well as doing corrections. *(Remaining mistakes are my own from 'fiddling'!).*

Wendy at CPI, for her prompt response to my printing request, and her interest in the project, and Martin and Stacey at CPI for their help and support in the past.

Gill for looking after Dodi when he comes to be clipped.

Joyce for providing Dodi's second home when we have to go somewhere that he can't go.

Christine, Martin & Tia, without Tia we may not have looked for Dodi.

Ray & Scooby, Dodi's best friends; especially Ray who always has a small piece of sausage in his pocket for Dodi. Ray is the only person Dodi can 'see' 50 yards away!

Margaret & Robert (Meg & Bob) Dodi's collie friends.

Jake a special doggy friend Dodi met in Essex, and his Mum who first suggested the idea of a book about Dodi's adventures.

Everyone locally who has taken an interest in Dodi's recovery and wellbeing.

About the Author

Dr.'Ella' Morgan was born in Singapore in 1949, the daughter of an army family. She and her brother travelled the world with their parents. Her mother died in 1972 at the incredibly young age of 42, 'Ella' had just begun her teaching career. She taught in a village primary school in East Anglia for 10 years and then worked with the local health authority teaching blind babies. This work led to her becoming the first director of a joint initiative respite care scheme *(Social Services and Mencap).* At the end of the project she returned to primary teaching as a deputy head teacher and subsequently became an LEA advisor for SEN, terminal illness and sensory impairment. From this comprehensive educational background 'Ella' became a university lecturer teaching research methodology and reflective practice. She was then appointed head of department for inservice modular degree programmes; simultaneously studying for and gaining a PhD in educational research philosophy. After moving from the south to Cumbria she became a freelance policy and practice research consultant working with a number of northern universities, and FE colleges and producing numerous research reports and FE teaching materials. 'Ella' retired from consultancy work two years ago to spend more time with Dennis, Dodi and the garden.

In collaboration with a 14 yr old suffering from school phobia 'Ella' wrote the very successful 'Fear & Longing' (*also published by Redstone Books in 2008).* She is currently working on two novels to be published in 2013.